Standing for Yourself

by Linda Kita-Bradley

Grass Roots Press

Standing up for Yourself
© 2018 Grass Roots Press
www.grassrootsbooks.net

All rights reserved. No part of this book may be reproduced or transmitted in any form or by any means, including photocopy, recording, or any information storage or retrieval system, without the prior written permission of the publisher.

Acknowledgements

Grass Roots Press acknowledges the financial support of the Government of Canada for our publishing activities.

Produced with the assistance of the Government of Alberta through the Alberta Multimedia Development Fund.

Editor: Dr. Pat Campbell
Photography: Susan Rogers
Book design: Lara Minja, Lime Design Inc.

Library and Archives Canada Cataloguing in Publication

Kita-Bradley, Linda, 1958–, author
        Standing up for yourself / Linda Kita-Bradley ; Susan Rogers, photographer.

(Soft skills at work)
ISBN 978–1–77153–225–9 (softcover)

        1. Readers for new literates. 2. Readers—Employee rights.
        3. Readers—Confidence. I. Rogers, Susan, 1952–, photographer II. Title.

PE1126.N43K5874 2018   428.6'2   C2017–906939–X

Part 1

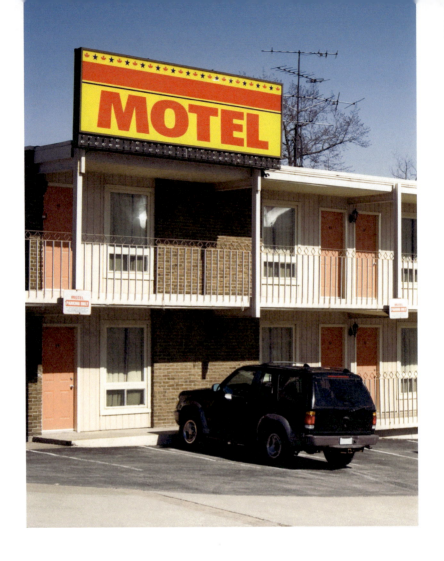

Nan works at a motel.

She cleans.

She uses a lot of cleaners.

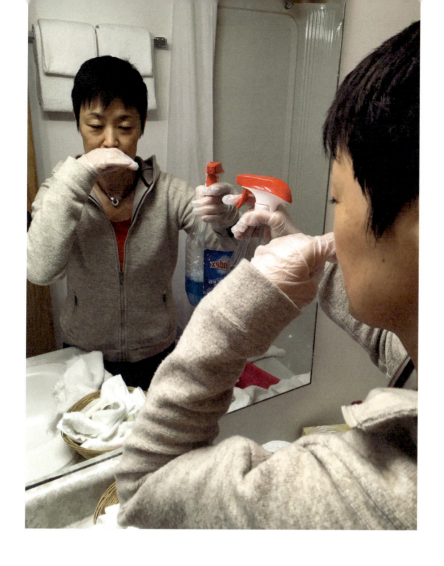

The cleaners are strong.

Nan wears gloves.

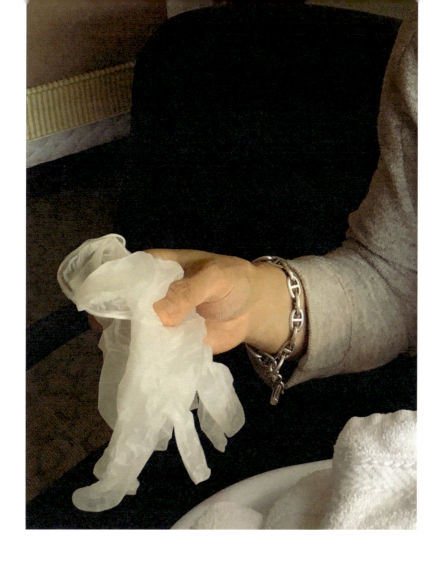

But the gloves are cheap.

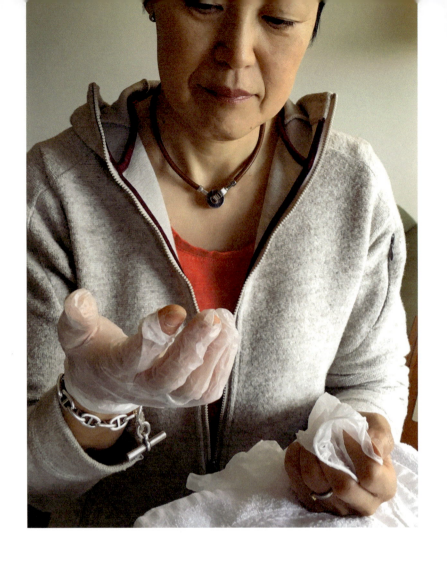

They rip and tear.

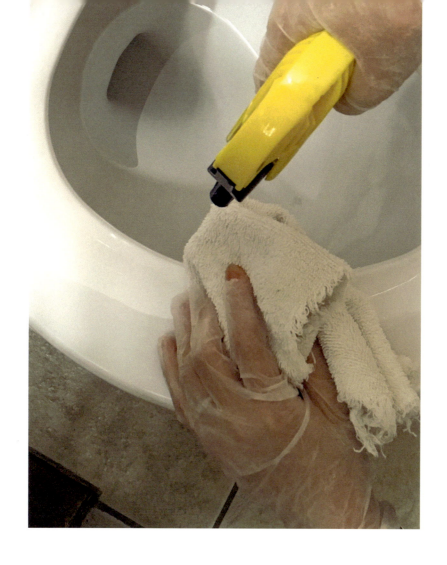

The cleaners go through the holes.

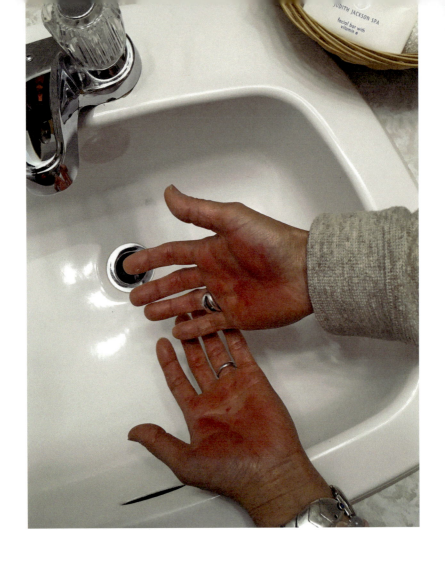

Nan has a rash.

Water makes her hands feel better.

Cream makes her hands feel better.

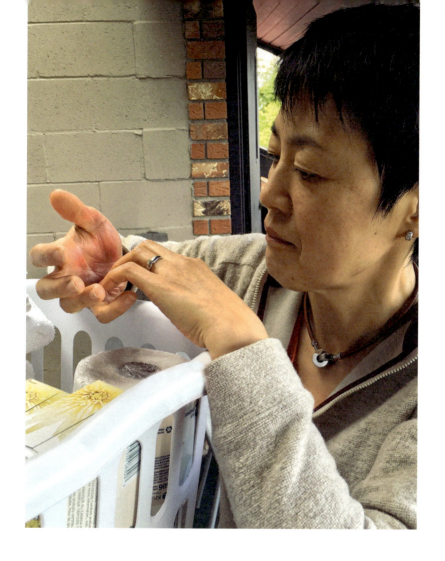

But the rash does not go away.
The rash is itchy.

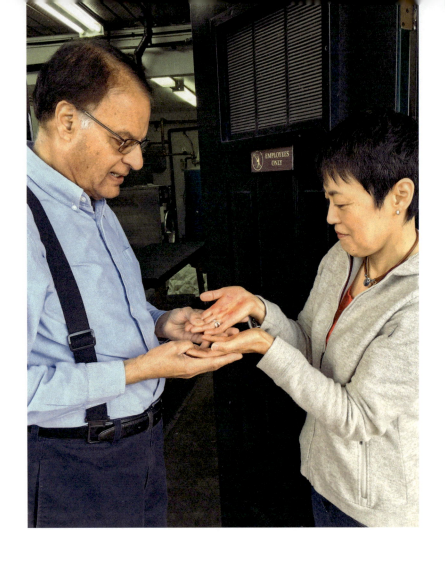

Nan shows her boss the rash.

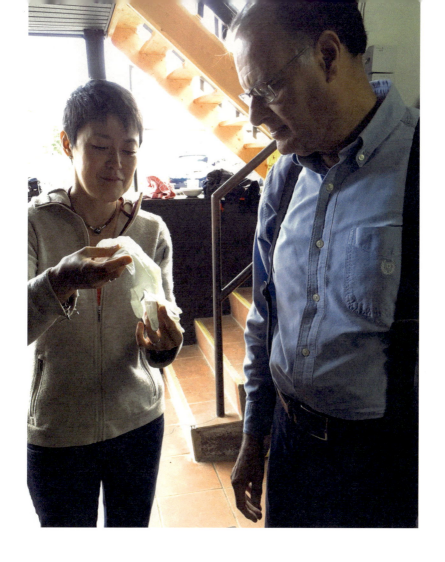

Nan shows her boss the gloves.
Nan says, "The gloves are cheap."

Nan's boss says, "Try another pair."

Her boss walks away.

Nan wants to say something.
But she says nothing.

She is afraid to stand up for herself.

Is she the only one with a rash?

Nan feels alone.

Nan buys her own gloves.

The rash goes away.

Talking About the Story

1. What does standing up for yourself mean?

    Why is it important to stand up for yourself?

2. Imagine you are Nan. Your boss does not want to help you.

    How do you feel?

3. In your opinion, why doesn't Nan stand up for herself?

Part 2

Read the next story about Nan.
How is it different from the first story?

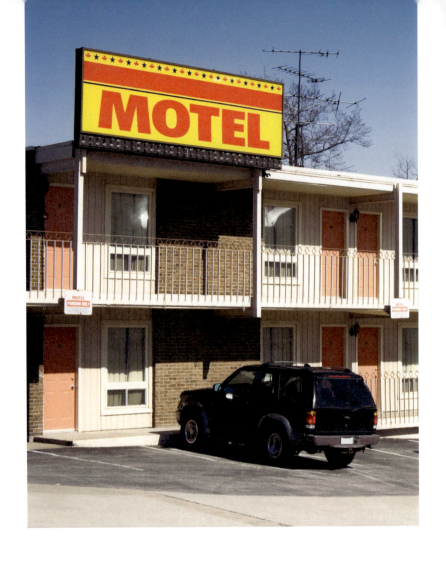

Nan works at a motel.

She cleans.

She uses a lot of cleaners.

The cleaners are strong.

Nan wears gloves.

But the gloves are cheap.

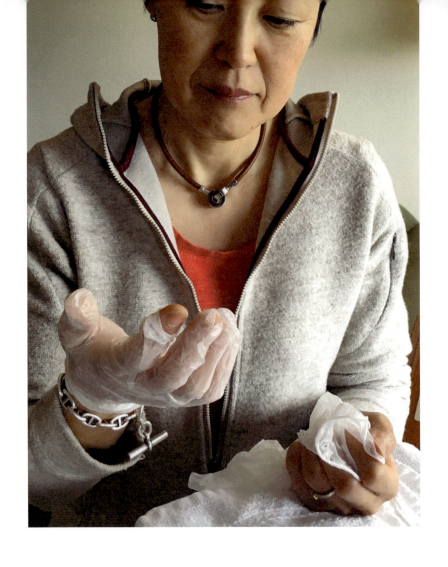

They rip and tear.

The cleaners go through the holes.

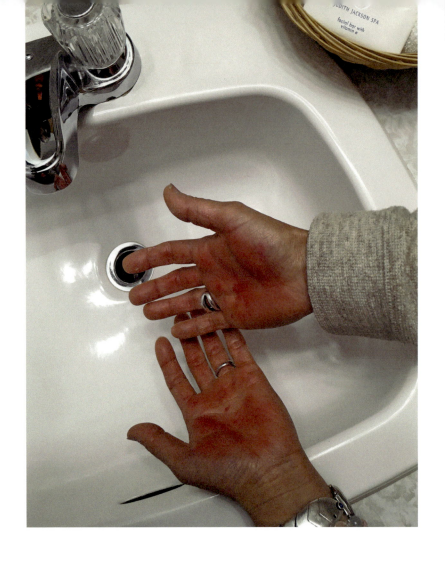

Nan has a rash.

Is she the only one with a rash?

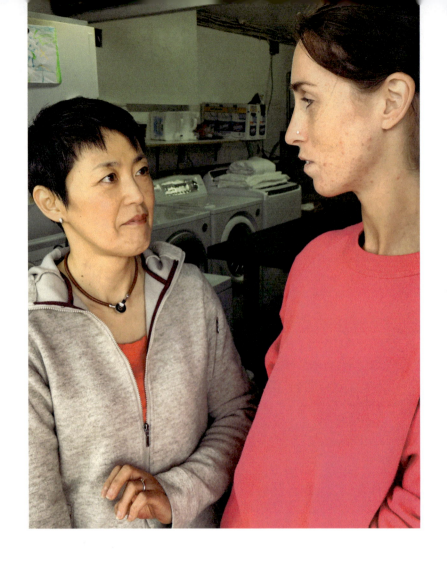

Nan talks to Sue.

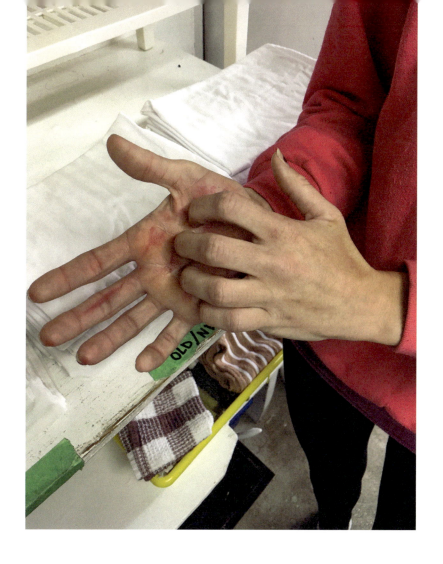

Sue has a rash, too.

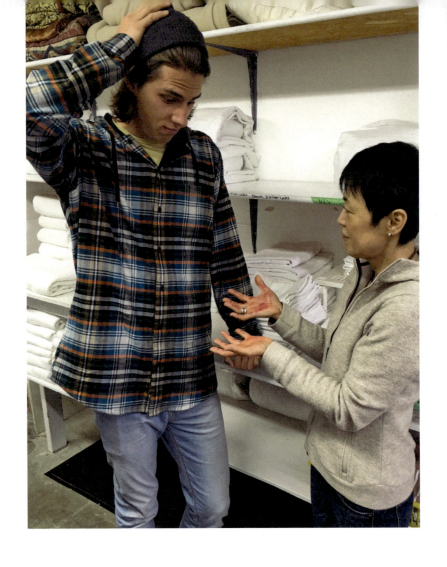

Nan shows Roy her rash.

Roy is surprised.
He does not have a rash.

But his eyes hurt all the time.

The staff talk to their boss.
Nan and Sue say, "Look at our rash."

Roy says, "My eyes hurt."

The boss listens to them.

The boss buys better gloves.

The boss buys safe cleaners.

Nan smiles.
She does not feel alone anymore.

Made in the USA
Columbia, SC
13 September 2024